Reuben Allerton

**Brook trout fishing**

Reuben Allerton

**Brook trout fishing**

ISBN/EAN: 9783337145712

Printed in Europe, USA, Canada, Australia, Japan

Cover: Foto ©Andreas Hilbeck / pixelio.de

More available books at **www.hansebooks.com**

# BROOK TROUT FISHING.

## AN ACCOUNT OF A TRIP

### OF THE

# Oquossoc Angling Association

## TO NORTHERN MAINE,

### In June, 1869.

# BY R. G. ALLERTON.

NEW YORK:

PRINTED BY FERRIS & BROWNE, 164 FULTON STREET,

For the Publisher, R. G. ALLERTON, 205 Broadway.

1869.

TO MY EXCELLENT FRIEND AND BROTHER ANGLER,

## GEORGE SHEPARD PAGE,

Of Stanley, N. J.,

WHOSE GOOD EXAMPLE AND CHRISTIAN INFLUENCE ARE KEENLY
APPRECIATED, AND WITH WHOM I HAVE SPENT MANY
DELIGHTFUL HOURS

AMONG THE SUNDAY-SCHOOL CHILDREN,

AND IN THE HAUNTS OF THE NOBLE TROUT OF MAINE,

THIS LITTLE WORK IS MOST AFFECTIONATELY
DEDICATED.

R. G. A.

New York, October, 1869.

# CONTENTS.

—•◆•—

# ILLUSTRATIONS.

# TROUTING.

BY G. SWEET.

When spring her vernal carpet spreads
And makes the meadows green,
And violets with their purple heads
On every side are seen,
O, then I love to wander out
Where rippling waters gleam,
And fish for sly and active trout
That haunt the flowing stream.

The bobolincoln's joyous notes
Sent forth while on the wing ;
And music from a thousand throats
Makes hill and valley ring.
The brilliant flowers, sweet and fair,
That lure the busy bee ;
The fragrant, fresh, and bracing air
All have their charms for me.

Some folks may love to lie and sleep
And have their morning dreams,
But I prefer to slily creep
Along the rushing streams,
With rod and line both light and strong,
And hooks of trusty steel ;
I'm happier as I trudge along,
Than any King can feel.

But then the crowning charm of all
(One need not have a doubt)
Is from the clear cold brook to haul
A mess of splendid trout.
With stealthy tread, and cautious cast,
The close watch on the line ;
The tug, that tells the fish is fast,
O, then, what joy is mine!

The rush, the check, the sudden flash
When first his side is seen,
With bending rod, and struggling splash
He's landed on the green ;
Now see his colors fresh and bright,
That shine like burnished gold,
The crimson red, the silvery white,
And form of fairest mould.

We gaze with pleasure on our prize,
A foot in length, or more,
As in the basket safe he lies
With others, full a score.
Of all the fish that swim about,
In River, Lake, or Sea,
None can compare with speckled trout,
None, half so dear to me.

Dedicated to R. G. A. with the respects of the Author.

# ABOUT

# Brook Trout Fishing.

THE following account, prepared by one of the party, is intended to describe some of the events of a remarkable Trout Fishing Excursion to the lakes and streams of northern Maine, in the month of June, 1869.

## THE OQUOSSOC ANGLING ASSOCIATION,

of which Mr. GEO. SHEPARD PAGE, of Stanley, N. J., is President, composed at present of thirty gentlemen of Maine, Massachusetts, New York, New Jersey and Pennsylvania, have purchased a large tract of land enclosing several fine trout ponds and streams in northern Maine; and a large house is now being erected for the accommodation of themselves, their wives and children. As a summer resort in the wild woods this locality will surpass anything of the kind in Maine, or in the Adirondacks of New York, in the glorious sport of brook trout fishing which it affords, and in its many facilities for agreeable camp life.

The fishing party this season, numbered eleven, all members of the Association, as follows:

JAY COOKE, Banker, Philadelphia.

H. C. FAHNESTOCK, of Jay Cooke & Co , New York.

GEO. F. BAKER, Cashier First National Bank, New York.

GEO. SHEPARD PAGE, of Page, Kidder & Co., New York.

LEWIS B. REED, Jr., of F. & L. B. Reed, Jr., New York.

J. D. BADGLEY, of Badgley & Mead, New York.

GEO. W. GILBERT, Security Insurance Co., New York.

R. G. ALLERTON, Treas. Goodyear's India Rubber Co., N. Y.

I. M. CUTLER, of Farmington, Maine

WM. P FRYE, Attorney General of Maine.

W. S. BADGER, Editor Maine Farmer, Augusta.

Numerous other angling parties visited the fishing grounds during the stay of the Oquossocs, and all were very successful in taking trout. Below will be found the names of a few of the angling gentlemen present:

F. G. WHITNEY, of Whitney & Rice, New York.

E. RICE, of Whitney & Rice, New York.

H. F. MARTIN, of New York.

R. J. BAILY, of Pennsylvania.

Rev. WM. R. TOMPKINS, of Wrentham, Mass.

H. M. MESSINGER, of Messinger, Moore & Co., New York.

A. R. McCOY, of Keese & McCoy, New York.

WM. MAXWELL, of Easton, Pennsylvania.

J. SANDS, of Randolph, Mass.

CHAS. G. ATKINS, Fish Commissioner of Maine.

JNO. M. ADAMS, Editor Eastern Argus, Portland, Maine.

" BIG INDIAN "
Chief of the Original Oquossocs.

" By Kennebago's dashing waters
Dwelt Oquossoc's fairest daughters."

## RED SPECKLED TROUT.

The trout taken by the party are the genuine *Red Speckled Brook Trout*, Lake Trout not being known in the locality. Many anglers will doubt that these trout, from their enormous size, are the genuine brook trout, but such they most assuredly are, Prof. Agassiz, the highest authority, having classed them as *Salmo fontinalis*.

The spots and tints are as beautiful as can be imagined; and the fish increase in beauty as they increase in size. They have all the recognized peculiarities of brook trout, such as square tails, small heads, the inside of the mouth black (instead of white, like lake trout); and lastly, the beautiful bright vermilion spots which characterize all brook trout.

Following is an exact account of the numbers and weights of thirty brook trout taken by eight of the party; average time of fishing about six days each. In this list none are mentioned under four pounds each, although an immense quantity of smaller ones were taken. It is, without doubt, the greatest catch of large brook trout by any one party, in the same time, ever known; and the world is challenged to pro-

duce a record that will surpass or even equal
the following:

## WEIGHTS AND NUMBERS OF THIRTY LARGE BROOK TROUT.

| | | | | | |
|---|---|---|---|---|---|
| 3 | Brook Trout, | - - | 4 | pounds | each. |
| 1 | " " | - - - | $4\frac{1}{4}$ | " | |
| 1 | " " | - - | $4\frac{1}{2}$ | " | |
| 2 | " " | - - - | $4\frac{3}{4}$ | " | each. |
| 3 | " " | - - | 5 | " | " |
| 1 | " " | - - - | $5\frac{1}{4}$ | " | |
| 4 | " " | - - | $5\frac{1}{2}$ | " | each. |
| 2 | " " | - - - | 6 | " | " |
| 2 | " " | - - | $6\frac{1}{2}$ | " | " |
| 2 | " " | - - - | $6\frac{3}{4}$ | " | " |
| 2 | " " | - - | 7 | " | " |
| 1 | " " | - - - | $7\frac{1}{4}$ | " | |
| 1 | " " | - - | $7\frac{1}{2}$ | " | |
| 3 | " " | - - - | 8 | " | each. |
| 1 | " " | - - | $8\frac{1}{2}$ | " | |
| 1 | " " | - - - | 9 | " | |

Making 30 Trout, total weight $181\frac{1}{4}$ lbs.,
averaging over 6 lbs. each.

The "taking" was pretty fairly divided among
the party; but a few items of individual skill
will be of interest.

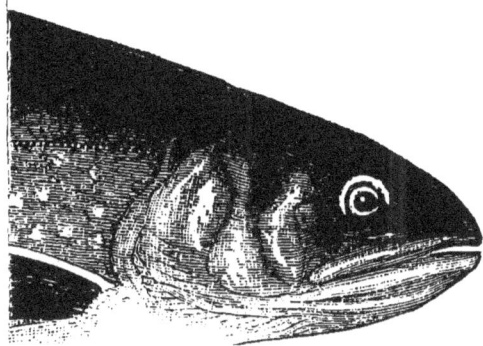

THE ANGLER'S PRIDE
BROOK TROUT. (Salmo fontinalis.)

Painted by Helen M. Findlay, expressly for R. G. A., from a living Speckled Trout, furnished by Mr. Geo. Shepard Page.

Mr. Cooke was fortunate enough to return to camp on the evening of June 2d, with a magnificent seven-and-a-half-pounder alive in his car, and two or three days later took this beautiful specimen of the finny tribe to his home near Philadelphia, where upon his arrival he gave a grand dinner, at which the "giant captive" was the attractive dish. The Press of Philadelphia was well represented on the occasion. Mr. C. on another day captured one of 3 lbs. and one of 4 lbs.

Mr. Reed took one $3\frac{1}{4}$ and one $7\frac{1}{4}$ lbs.

Mr. Page one 3, one 4, and one 6 lbs.

Mr. Baker one $2\frac{1}{2}$, and one $4\frac{3}{4}$ lbs.

Mr. Gilbert one 3, one $3\frac{1}{4}$, one $4\frac{1}{4}$, one $5\frac{1}{4}$, and one $6\frac{3}{4}$ lbs.

Mr. Fahnestock one $2\frac{1}{2}$, one $3\frac{1}{2}$, one $4\frac{3}{4}$, and one 5 lbs.

Mr. Badgley two of $5\frac{1}{2}$ lbs. each, one $6\frac{3}{4}$ lbs., one 8 lbs., and one 9 lbs., making five trout, averaging nearly 7 lbs. each.

Mr. Badgley's nine pounder ranks as the largest trout taken this year. Mr. B. caught during one day, in less than two hours, three of those given in his list weighing $6\frac{3}{4}$, 8, and 9 lbs.; total weight $23\frac{3}{4}$ lbs.

Mr. Allerton, who remained considerably longer than any of the other gentlemen, caught as follows:

Two of 5 lbs. each, two of 5½, one of 6, two of 6½, two of 7, one of 7½, two of 8, and one of 8½, making thirteen trout, weighing 86 lbs. and averaging 6 lbs. 10 oz. each. Mr. A. caught, in addition to the above, twenty-seven trout, weighing 61 lbs., from one lb. up to five lbs. each, averaging 2¼ lbs.; also, 207 weighing 87¼ lbs., under one lb. each, averaging 6¾ ozs.; total catch, 247 trout weighing 234¼ lbs., averaging nearly one pound each.

The best twenty trout of the last-mentioned angler's taking, averaged 5½ lbs. each, and the best forty 3 lbs. 11 oz. each. Of these trout he caught four in three-quarters of an hour on the afternoon of June 22d, that being his last half day's fishing, as he left for home next morning. The four weighed respectively 5, 5½, 6, and 8 lbs., making a total of 24½ lbs. of trout caught in three-quarters of an hour, a very satisfactory "wind up" to the grandest fishing excursion confessedly ever made by him.

The trout caught this season of 7 to 9 lbs. measured from 25 to 28 inches in length, and from 14 to 20 inches around. The tails, when spread, measured from 5½ to 8 inches across.

## MODE OF TAKING THE TROUT.

In the spring nearly all the large trout are taken by trolling and still-fishing, the live minnow being chiefly used for bait. They are taken in the lakes, in deep water, with light tackle, some using even fly-rods with thin lines, and very small hooks.

## CAPTURE OF A LARGE TROUT.

A brief description of the capture of an 8½ pound speckled trout will no doubt be read with interest by all who are fond of this rare sport.

On Saturday afternoon, June 5th, as we, the writer and friend Badgley, and our Guide, were pursuing our usual occupation of trolling around a favorite point where the water is so deep that the shy trout are not disturbed by the passing boat, we were all startled by the very sudden "strike" of something heavy in the form of a goodly fish many feet below and behind the boat. It proved to be the narrator who was in luck this time; and now for the story—but to what end, since no written words of his can recall the wild excitement of the moment? He only wishes that all who read this had been there to have shared in his enjoyment.

Having a good trolling rod with multiplying reel containing 600 feet of very small but very strong linen line, with 150 feet paid out, a trusty single gut leader and small hook, and holding our rod firmly, the boat moving moderately along, all in readiness and very eager for a strike, it came all at once, and for downright heaviness and determination on the part of the fish not to budge or be moved one inch, it far surpassed all strikes of past experience. The jerking of the arms gave the writer a sensation not unlike that occasioned by the jerking motion of a railway car when the locomotive suddenly starts.

The trout was surely well hooked, and by himself, too. The boat was instantly stopped and by trusty David turned broadside on. By this time the fish had sufficiently recovered from his astonishment to take a turn or two, and heavy turns and ugly twists he did take for a few moments, when he suddenly made for the bottom where he lay, sullen and immovable, but not until he had run off about 200 feet of line, fortunately well out into the lake, where the Guide quickly followed. We were now in first-rate shape, " *all quiet on the Cuptomac,* " and the trout sure to remain where he was for some time.

Friend Badgley taking note of the time to know how long a job we were in for, concluded to light up one of his choice Havanas and see if he could smoke him out; and David was all prepared to test the capacity of the landing-net.

When the trout "hitched on," several boats were near at hand, and the occupants were decidedly interested spectators, plying up and down and about us, watching for the *denouement*.

After thirty minutes sulking, the coveted denizen of the deep took another turn, and off went more line, the reel buzzing away like a bag full of mosquitoes.

And now for the last chapter. After repeated runs and spasmodic jerks and shakes, the conquered warrior came up alongside like a lamb, looking completely exhausted. He was now easily run into the net, head first, lifted on board, and laid out flat upon the seat of the boat. Mr. B. referring to his watch pronounced the time occupied in the capture to be just forty-nine minutes; less time could not have secured him. He was indeed a magnificent fellow to look at, richly speckled, with colors as beautiful as the rainbow.

All the boats now came rushing up, some parties calling out lustily, "How much does he weigh?" which was immediately ascertained to be 8½ pounds. He was rather a short trout, being only 25 inches in length, but measured around full 17 inches. He soon recovered after being placed in the fish car, and when transferred to the camp car in the running stream, he was as lively as ever, not being injured in the least. Several days later he was served up in fine style, as described hereafter. Some of the parties, present at this defeat of one of the *heavy weights*, will not soon forget the scene, and all will be sure to remember the

### TERRIFIC STORM

of thunder and lightning, wind and rain, which followed immediately after, a description of which the writer is not able to give, commensurate with the grandeur of the event, but will refer the reader to the most graphic account he can find of some other "big blow," written by one equal to the work.

"Fiercely raged the King of Storms."

## FLY FISHING.

Fly fishing for large trout is not very successful in the spring anywhere, but late in summer
and in September the very largest trout are
taken in Maine, in the streams, with the artificial fly and with the most delicate rods in use,
some weighing as light as six ounces.

A good many small trout from $\frac{1}{4}$ to 3 lbs.
each, were taken by our party this season with
the artificial fly.

It is hardly necessary to say that the writer,
in common with the others of the party, prefer
this mode to all other methods of taking
trout, but in order to enjoy the exquisite sport
of taking very large trout in this fashion, it
is necessary that they should show some dis-
position to rise at your flies after having made
a few hundred casts; but as all trout above 3
lbs. positively declined to take the slightest
notice of our repeated attentions, the writer,
with others decided to adopt the next most
enjoyable style of trout fishing, viz.: trolling
with a live minnow; and the extraordinary
success we met with in taking the large growth,
reconciled us in a great degree to this method
of angling. But first, last, and all the time, fly-

THE GENTLE PASSION STRONG IN YOUTH.

fishing for trout is, *par excellence, the sport* for all true anglers, and in the proper season it will be prosecuted by the Oquossocs with vigor and no doubt with great success.

## TROUT PACKING.

A great many trout are packed in birch bark, ice and saw-dust, and taken away to families and friends. Many boxes have been brought to New York this season, the fish arriving in excellent condition. One lot caught by the writer, including four trout, weighing 23 pounds—one of them an eight pounder—after arriving in New York, were re-packed and sent to Dutchess County, N. Y., where there are but few people, even of the oldest inhabitants, who had ever seen a brook trout weighing over three pounds.

Three boxes of trout, caught by the writer also, were sent to New York to his brother, Mr. Geo. M. Allerton, who took great pleasure in distributing them among friends, all of whom testify that the fish were most delicious and had a remarkably fresh flavor, an exceedingly rare quality in brook trout as usually served in New York City, and a proof that Maine Guides know how to pack trout in such a manner that they will be choice eating even after several days of transportation.

The three boxes contained about 100 trout, weighing in the aggregate 150 pounds, varying from half a pound to eight pounds each. Their exhibition produced great astonishment, as many who witnessed the sight had never been accustomed to see brook trout weighing over two or three pounds. Nearly all readily admitted that these specimens went ahead of any thing they had even heard of before, as to size and beauty; but one or two made a show of doubting that they were the real brook trout, calling them salmon, salmon trout, lake trout, &c., or anything but brook trout, so reluctant were they to admit fairly, that their great 3 or 4 pound trout, caught some forty or fifty years ago, should at last be thrown so completely in the shade; but it was of no use, "seeing was believing," and the situation had to be accepted.

The writer presented an 8 pounder to Dr. Alex. B. Mott, who was not a little surprised at the size of the gift. The Doctor afterwards told how he had him served up for supper, warmed up for breakfast, hashed up for dinner, and bade him farewell only at the fourth meal.

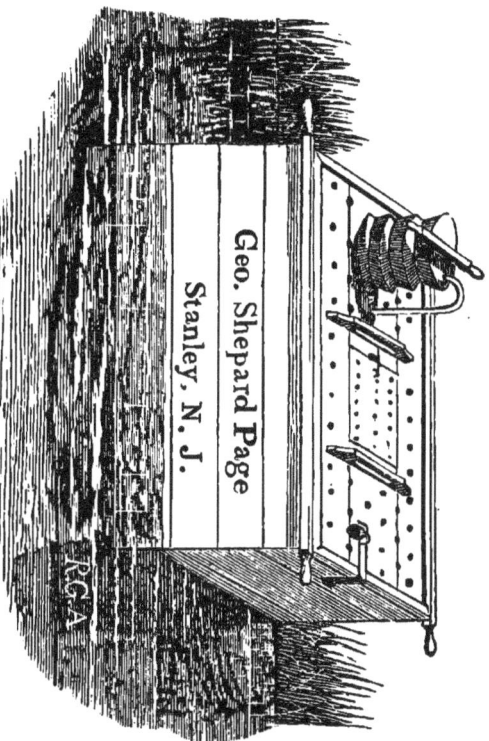

(Sketched by R. G. A., from memory.)

TANK FOR CARRYING LIVE TROUT, KNOWN AS PAGE'S RATTLESNAKE BOX.

These large trout baked or boiled are most delicious, but for frying the small ones are much preferable.

## TRANSPORTATION OF LIVE TROUT.

Mr. Page, the President of the Angling Association, took to the fishing grounds a very peculiar box, made expressly for transporting live trout to his place in New Jersey. It is lined with sponge to prevent injury to the fish, and has a sliding cover, fitting tightly, with numerous air holes. An air pump is attached, and a man is employed to accompany the box, whose duty it is to supply fresh air to the trout, the water not being changed for the entire distance. Mr. Page this season took to his artificial trout ponds in Stanley, N. J., sixty-two trout, in the above manner, weighing from $\frac{1}{4}$ to 3 pounds each—only two of his take of sixty-four dying on the way. The said box caused considerable amusement at the railway stations, as it was supposed to contain rattlesnakes. Some of the railroad employees of Celtic lineage actually refused to assist in moving the cage.

## REV. MR. MURRAY'S NEW BOOK.

The writer having read the Rev. Mr. Murray's recent work, "*Murray's Adventures in the Ad-*

*irondack Wilderness,*" and having made five trips through said wilderness, traversing nearly every important lake and river therein, feels himself authorized, in accordance with the requests of fishermen friends, to refer to some portions of the book, for he must say, with due respect to the author of a very entertaining narrative, that he cannot quite agree with all his statements concerning the Adirondack and the Maine wildernesses.

Mr. Murray's book, if accepted as a guide, will surely cause much bitter disappointment, as much that is therein described has existence only in the imagination of the enthusiastic author. He has of course not meant to misrepresent anything, but the effect will be the same. All who are thoroughly familiar with the Adirondacks will unite in saying that the book, as a guide, is quite unreliable. A complete review of the book being out of the question here, some of the principal points of difference are selected for notice.

The portion of Maine visited by our party this season is as lovely as one could desire, and with one exception, quite equal to any portion of the *North Woods* of New York. There are many beautiful lakes and streams in the Adirondacks, Raquette River being probably the most beautiful stream in any wilderness. The brook trout fishing is excellent, but not by any means equal to that of certain portions of Maine; and Mr. Murray would be among the first to admit the fact had he been with us last June. Where we were is no lumbered district, and no logs with the owner's "mark" on, were seen. The writer, with a valued friend, three years ago last June, journeyed from Lake Pleasant, Hamilton County, N. Y., over many lakes and rivers, including the Blue Mountain lakes and Raquette Lake and River, and over numerous carries, (one of thirteen miles,) to Martin's, on the Lower Saranac, a distance of about 150 miles, and he is enforced to say that the lumberman's axe *had* been known in the Adirondack Wilderness; for on nearly the whole route may be encountered numerous logs bearing the owner's "mark," particularly in the Raquette and Saranac Rivers, as well as in the Saranac Lakes, Tupper's Lake, and all about Paul Smith's, at St. Regis. Apollos Smith, called for short "Pol.," has finally settled down into being addressed as Paul Smith. The Rev. Dr. S. H. Coxe, of Utica, with whom the writer camped

last year at Tupper's Lake, relates once visiting
Paul Smith's, and was soon after anxiously in-
quiring, "where was Paul and where was Apollos?" supposing there were two landlords, the
sign reading Apollos, and the guests familiarly
saying Paul.

Mr. Murray speaks of his house as the St.
James of the woods, which is true and praise
enough, and Paul himself is a great favorite.

Bartlett's, between upper Saranac and Round
Lake, is an excellent place to stop at, and one
can always be sure of every attention by the
kind proprietor and his wife.

Martin's, on the Lower Saranac, is one of the
best places in the Adirondacks for comfort, good
table and attention by the host and hostess.

Graves's, near the head of Tupper's Lake,
must not be omitted here. "Billy Graves," for-
merly of Boston, with his excellent wife, are de-
serving of all praise for the way in which they
treat their guests.

It should be mentioned here, that in May and
June, when the water is high, the logs are met
with, as that is the season for running them.
Mr. Murray visiting the Wilderness in July,
August and September, of course would not be

apt to meet much in the way of floating timber; but it is a fact that thousands of logs are to be seen in the Adirondack Wilderness proper, although many sections, such as Raquette Lake and portions of Raquette River, as well as many of the smaller lakes and streams are free from these nuisances.

Mr. Murray will no doubt be ready to admit that Raquette Falls, and Raquette River below the Falls, the Saranac Lakes, Tupper's Lake, &c., are not to be considered as the over-hunted borders of the Adirondacks, but may safely be set down as portions of the Wilderness proper. He says that "no fires have blackened the hills in the Adirondacks." The writer's experience is different, he having seen many sad traces of the wanton "Incendiary of the woods," a creature who should be well warmed when caught.

No doubt plenty of booms, logs, slabs and saw-dust can be seen in certain parts of Maine, as they surely can be in certain parts of the Adirondacks. Near Paul Smith's, for instance, there is an immense saw-mill, turning out loads of saw-dust to choke the trout. Where our party went in Maine no saw-mill was to be seen, and all the "*tramping*" we had to do was one rather pleasant carry of two miles.

As for black flies, (which Mr. Murray thinks no great annoyance,) they are plentiful in Maine, and they are plentiful in the Adirondacks too; and in the latter region their bite is sharper than in the former. If any one can pass through Marion River, Raquette River, Forked Lake, Long Lake, &c., in June, or early in July, and not be seriously vexed by the black fly, he is indeed most fortunate—a bitter experience proving the contrary in the writer's case, and in that of a companion fisherman who will give melancholy testimony to the fact, yet Mr. Murray says of the black fly, "I regard it as one of the most harmless and least vexatious of the insect family."

While on the subject of black flies, the following extract will not be out of place, agreeing as it does so perfectly with the experience of the writer and of many of his friends, who have been in the habit of visiting fishing grounds infested by these insects.

SPORTING SKETCHES BY AN OLD ANGLER.

*From Stewart's Quarterly Magazine for April, 1869, published in St. John, New Brunswick.*

"The only drawback to our complete comfort, was the pertinacious attacks of black flies, midges and mosquitoes.

Our friend's hook having caught on a rock, he is endeavoring to get it loose, and what with wading as deep as he dare, and reaching out with his landing net staff, he is having a severe trial of his patience, the hook all the time being several feet beyond his reach.

These pests are the Anglers, "bête noir." The midge and mosquito are simply annoying, but the small black fly is perfectly maddening to those who are unfortunate enough to possess a sensitive epidermis. Pertinaciously they persist in their merciless attacks, and find their way into ears, eyes and nostrils, and through every unguarded aperture in the clothing. Their bite generally brings blood, and always leaves an intolerable itching, which the slightest irritation serves only to increase. After a time the blood appears to become inoculated with their virus, and their bite causes but little pain or annoyance. The initiatory process, however, is far from agreeable, and to some persons quite destroys the pleasure of forest life."

Mosquitoes are plenty in both regions, and about equally venomous. As for the midges, or gnats, none were seen this trip in Maine, but they were met with in the Adirondacks in countless millions; and all Mr. Murray says in their disfavor is well deserved. Mr. Murray gives the distance from Keeseville to Martin's as 56 miles. The writer having asked the distance a great many times of different persons, nearly all agreed in placing it at about eight miles less, yet it might be 56, as not much reliance can be placed on individual estimates of country distances, each one having a favorite estimate of his own.

Mr. Murray recalls many familiar spots, particularly Blue Mountain Lake, the most beautiful of all, the lakes of Maine not excepted.

It is a very rare thing to take a brook trout in the Adirondacks as heavy as five pounds, three pounds being considered a large trout there; it is quite common in Maine to take them weighing seven and eight pounds each, sometimes even nine pounds, and one of ten pounds was taken by Mr. Page about two years since, and can now be seen stuffed, in a glass case, at his office, No. 139 Maiden Lane, New York.

Mr. Murray, on page 137, gives the length of the largest trout he caught at 17¾ inches. The Maine trout, weighing from seven to nine pounds, will measure from 25 to 28 inches in length; and Mr. Page's ten pounder is just 30 inches long.

Lake trout are plenty in the Adirondacks, and some as heavy as 15 to 20 pounds are taken, but compared to the red speckled fellows they are common and unattractive to the eye. Every time you take a trout on the Maine fishing grounds visited by our party, he is sure to be a red speckled beauty. Many fish are caught in certain portions of Maine and other adjacent states, weighing from 10 to 20 pounds, and by some called speckled trout; speckled they are no doubt, but Brook Trout they surely are not.

As to boats, those of the Saranac and Long

Lake are models of beauty and speed. Maine is much behind the Adirondacks in this matter, but she will soon improve, as a contract is now being filled for quite a number of new boats, to be constructed on the grounds by an experienced builder, and there will be some improvements made over even the Saranacers.

The landing net is generally used in the Adirondacks for all small fish, but when it comes to the large ones, and particularly the lake trout, they are, in many cases, mercilessly "gaffed," a most unnecessary way of securing a trout.

In Maine nothing but the landing net is used, even for the largest fish, and the trout are not hammered on the head with a club, and thrown into the bottom of the boat to shrivel up or be crushed with the heavy boot, but placed in a neat car attached to the stern of the boat, where they are kept alive until the return to camp, when they are transferred to more roomy cars, which are kept submerged in the running stream. They are thus kept alive as long as required, and may be dressed for the table or to send home as soon as they have ceased flopping, a manifest advantage, as the trout are thus eaten as fresh as they possibly can be, which every lover of fresh fish will acknowledge to be of great importance. By this method all waste is done away with, something that cannot be too highly commended.

The writer would not seek to deprive the Adirondacks of one particle of their glory as a "sportsmen's paradise," knowing well what a delightful place it is to spend a summer vacation in, and knowing too that the fishing there is excellent; all that is desired in speaking upon this subject is, not to let "Old Maine" suffer too much, which she might do were Mr. Murray's book taken for more than it is—a very entertaining work, compiled by a gentleman of romantic temperament and vivid imagination, and very much in love with the Adirondacks. We would indeed be ungrateful, if, forgetful of our glorious sport and the beautiful surroundings of the haunts of our finny favorites, we had not a grateful word to say in defence of the attractions of the Old Pine Tree State.

Since the foregoing reference to Mr. Murray's book was put in type, numerous paragraphs in the daily papers have appeared, reflecting very severely on Mr. Murray for misleading so many tourists, who, following his advice, went to

THE MONARCH OF MAINE.

the Adirondack Wilderness in search of health
and sport. The accounts which gave rise to the
criticisms are no doubt exaggerated, but they
all agree that the disappointment is universal.
We are of course not surprised, knowing how
limited the accommodation is in the Adirondack
region, and how all chance of comfort and enjoyment must have departed with the pressure
of numbers. Those who have been in the wilderness and are posted, can again go there and
meet with reasonable success in fishing and
hunting, but those who go for the first time,
without the company of an experienced friend,
will meet with poor success, and make up their
minds that the Adirondack region is a humbug,
while such is really not the case, for there is
plenty of sport to be had, but *reliable* inform-
ation must first be obtained.

If the Adirondacks have been overrun with
thousands of tourists this summer, as the papers
say they have, it is natural that they should
feel hard toward Mr. Murray, yet they are
themselves to blame in a great measure, for
swallowing the book entire and then bolting for
the woods, without previously consulting some
friend who was able to post them correctly.

As to ladies visiting the wilderness, a few may do so safely and comfortably, if accompanied by an experienced protector, who has been at least two trips to the region proposed to be visited. As yet a few only can find accommodation, and these must be prepared to "rough it."

The writer, after three trips to the Adirondacks, ventured to take his wife there, (He has been positively forbidden to allude to this circumstance, but has decided to run the risk and take the consequences.) and she enjoyed the trip amazingly. We went in on the 20th of May, two years since, had a very delightful excursion, remained three weeks, caught plenty of trout, camped out for variety on Raquette River, and met Governor Fenton and party at Martin's and Bartlett's. We spent a portion of our time in company with the Governor, which added to the pleasure of our trip exceedingly.

Any one proposing to visit the Adirondack Wilderness, should procure a map of the region, and the best one is Dr. W. W. Ely's, published by Colton. Directions as to routes, &c., accompany the map, and they are correct as far as it is possible to make them so.

There have been many books published of late years on fish and fishing in American waters, but of them all, so far as the writer's observation extends, the "American Angler's Book," by Thaddeus Norris, deservedly stands at the head. Mr. Norris understands his subject thoroughly, at least that is the opinion of many, competent to judge, and his book with one or two unimportant exceptions, is accepted by nearly all anglers as authority on fish and fishing. What he says in reference to the Adirondack region may be depended upon with entire confidence. We will now leave the Adirondack subject for other interesting matter.

## OQUOSSOC.

As stately as his mountain pine
　　Here, once, Oquossoc's chieftain stood,
And with his barbéd spear transfixed
　　The nimble tenants of the flood.
Full many a year the rushing stream
　　The brave Oquossoc's praises sang;
Full many a time these forest aisles
　　With stern Oquossoc's prowess rang.

No longer glides his swift canoe
　　Adown the tumbling mountain wave.
The moaning waters chant his dirge,
　　The long grass droops above his grave.
No younger hand has grasped anew
　　The barbéd spear that his let fall;
For to the Happy Fields have fled,
　　Oquossoc's people, one and all.

The white man claims both hill and flood;
　　The pine tree falls before his steel;
The river broad, the forest aisles,
　　Are pathways for the rushing wheel.
Still, as he moves with giant pace
　　And ceaseless cries, "I am not done!"
The Red Man yields him hope and home
　　Save that *beyond* the setting sun.

To those of his readers who need an apology that he permitted himself to perpetrate
this Indian cry, the writer most penitently tenders one. To him as to Silas Wegg, the
transition from prose to verse, for once, was easy, and he slid thereinto. It is his first
attempt, and considering the difficulty he had in keeping his FEET he thinks it will be his
last. This assurance he trusts will reassure the reader "whose soul is not to music
tuned," and who is not desirous to hear more of "Lo! the Poor Indian."
　　Furthermore, there is no extra charge for this. If he had said this at first, probably
no apology had been necessary.

## SABBATH IN CAMP.

A most interesting Sabbath was spent at our camping ground. The Rev. Mr. Tompkins of Wrentham, Mass., and the Rev. Mr. Morrill of Maine, who were present on a trouting excursion, conducted the services, four gentlemen of the Oquossoc Association acting as choir. A rude pulpit consisting of a barrel, two boxes and a plank, was improvised and made agreeable to the eye by having Mr. Reed's traveling shawl spread over the whole, and adorned with beautiful wild flowers. The congregation numbered thirty-eight persons, and was composed of the residents of the sparsely settled country and the tourists, among whom were several noted gentlemen. All were deeply impressed with the services of this *meeting in the woods,* held in a lovely spot, suggestive of communings with Nature's God.

Mr. John M. Adams, a very agreeable gentleman, Editor of the *Daily Eastern Argus* of Portland, was present on the above day and was so well pleased with all he saw, including the ascent of a high mountain by eight gentlemen, that he afterwards printed an extended account of his trip, in his journal.

PAGE'S OQUOSSOC OWL.—The Pet of the Camp.

## GRAND TROUT SUPPER.

A Grand Trout Supper was given by the writer, to nine gentlemen, including those of the members of the Association, who had not yet departed. Several States were represented. Having two trout of his own catching, one of 6½ and one of 8½ lbs., it was decided to have them sacrificed and served up on the spot. It taxed the resources of the establishment severely to do this thing, but all difficulties being overcome, at 8 o'clock the comely pair were brought in, heads on, baked and flooded with rich sweet cream obtained from the settlement, and stuffed with all manner of good things, including pork and onions, certainly not to be despised in the woods. They were cooked to a turn, and all were in raptures over the big trout feast, which was filled out with a great variety of good things brought from the cities, including canned vegetables, fruits, &c. Privilege was granted by the manager of the camp for the guests to throw their fish bones and potato skins under the table if they desired, but, be it recorded, this liberality was not taken advantage of. As all the party did full justice to this late and heavy supper, next morning there were but few who had not been visited by queer dreams and night-mare apparitions in which many strange and odd looking fish flopped in every direction before their troubled eyes. The following cut represents as nearly as possible, one of the *scaly* fellows, seen in the visions of the night.

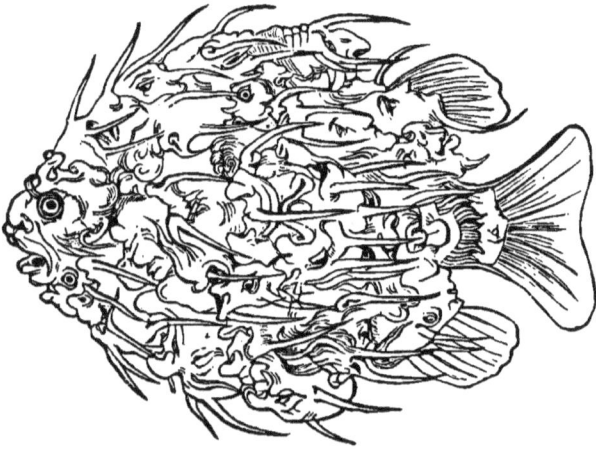

A QUEER FISH.

# GRAND
# TROUT SUPPER

GIVEN BY

## R. G. ALLERTON.

## BILL OF FARE.

*(As furnished for publication, by Mr. E. Rice.)*

### LACKAWANNA HOTEL,     C. T. Richardson, Prop'r.

*NORTHERN MAINE,*

## Thursday, June 10th, 1869.

### SOUP.

Tomato.       Ox Tail.

### FISH.

Two Brook Trout weighing 15 lbs.,* stuffed and baked in
Cream.

### MEATS.

Boiled Ham.     Corned Beef.     Fried Pork.

### VEGETABLES.

Fried Potatoes.      Boiled Potatoes.
Green Peas.     Tomatoes.
Bermuda Onions.

*These two Trout were caught by Mr. R. G. Allerton.

(OVER.)

# RELISHES.

Sardines.                    Horse Radish.
        Chow Chow.           Pickles.

# PASTRY.

Doughnuts.                   Sponge Cake.
        Apple Pie.

# BREAD.

White Bread.                         Toast.
        Hard Tack.

# Napkins.                   Toothpicks.
Birch Bark.                  Trout Ribs.

# FLUIDS.

Coffee.                              Tea.
        Kennebago Pura.

## Gentlemen Present at the Trout Supper.

| | |
|---|---|
| F. G. WHITNEY, | Massachusetts, |
| E. RICE, | New York, |
| I. M. CUTLER, | Maine, |
| WM. MAXWELL, | Pennsylvania, |
| H. F. MARTIN, | New York, |
| A. R. McCOY, | New Jersey, |
| J. SANDS, | Massachusetts, |
| R. J. BAILY, | Pennsylvania, |
| R. G. ALLERTON, | New York. |

## CAPTURE OF A LOON—A TRUE STORY.

On the return trip of the writer, while being rowed over a lake nine miles long, by his guide, a Loon, a bird noted for its wildness, was seen upon the shore sitting on a rock. At first it was thought to be upon its nest, but this proved to be a mistake. Rowing cautiously up to where it sat, we were allowed to land our boat directly in front of it, when the guide, knowing his business, stepped out very carefully and creeping up within reach, grasped the feathered beauty by the neck, and,—he was our bird. It proved to be a beautiful male specimen and in this instance must have been more than ordinarily "loony." Why he allowed himself to be caught it is difficult to say, as he had not been hurt in the least as far as we could ascertain. He appeared tolerably well and exceedingly strong, particularly in the beak, or as might truly be said, in his double set of Wade & Butcher Razors, which the Loon uses so well in "cutting up" small fry. In this instance he succeeded, in an unguarded moment, in closing the aforesaid Razors on the finger of a certain victim, but not the guide, (oh no indeed! he knew better,) and when closed (on the aforesaid finger,) quick as a flash, very tight and very sharp, somebody roared and jumped in a perpendicular direction as high as his Loonship would let him. The finger was released by the biter almost immediately, cut to the bone and bleeding profusely, and is not entirely healed to this day. A rubber band placed around a Loon's bill is a good thing, and it was applied in this case—this razor case—but as we have said unfortunately too late to prevent mischief. Placing a fish-basket strap around the Loon's wings, and with the band on his nose, he was now ready to set out on his travels by the stage, perched upon Mr. W's traveling bag, but owing to his general uneasiness and the inconvenience of his presence to other passengers, it was finally decided to leave him on the way. Fortunately meeting a very kind man, (Post-master of a village, but not one of A. J's as far as known,) who was in want of a Loon, and who promised to treat him well, two men were at once made happy by one bird, for he was set free in the P. M's Loon pond.

### BEAR STORIES, &C.

The only merit claimed for these memoranda, is their entire accordance with facts. No romantic "bear stories," nor "ghost stories, etc.," are

*( Sketched by R. G. A. )*
LOON CAUGHT AT OQUOSSOC LAKE.

indulged in, and not ten cents worth of tendency to fiction can be proved against the entire narrative. The loon story is literally true, every bit and bite of it. The only approach to a "bear story" shall be this, and for its truthfulness several gentlemen are ready to vouch. A real live black bear, and a good sized one too, was actually shot not far from our camp, the skin was soon after nailed up to dry, (see frontispiece,) and eventually went to the state of New Jersey, where another "Page" will relate the same bear story to wondering listeners of tender years.

OQUOSSOC BLACK BEAR.

This cut is here introduced on the lamb-page, in order that we may be forever reminded that—

> Mary had a little lamb,
> Its fleece was white as snow, &c., &c.

For the remainder of this charming poem, consult "Page on the Lamb," 12mo. sheep, published by Shepard.

MARY'S LAMB IN ITS INFANCY.

## THE MAINE PEOPLE.

In this account of a trip to Maine, it becomes a very pleasant duty to place on record our agreeable experience of its people. Wherever we traveled we were treated in the most hospitable manner by all, and it is only truth to say, that for kindness, sobriety and true friendship, the Maine people cannot be surpassed. As far as the writer learned, not one intoxicated man was seen by the party during the trip. The Maine law certainly works well in the land of its origin.

## INTERESTING EVENTS.

Before closing this narrative mention must be made of certain interesting events in connection with the trouting excursion, referring more particularly to Mr. Cooke and to Mr. Page, than whom no two more agreeable, friendly and really good Christian men can be found, in a fishing party or out of it. Mr. Cooke is most kind and generous wherever he goes, paying special attention to the little children, and to Sunday-schools and Churches. He presented libraries to the Sunday-schools of one of the villages through which we passed, Mr. Page doing the same at another village. Both of these gentlemen are

COUNTRY SCHOOL.

deeply interested in Sunday-schools and do a great deal for these Christianizing Institutions at their homes. Mr. Cooke has a very large school (some 400 scholars, if correctly remembered,) and Mr. Page has 170 little ones gathered in, and in a mere hamlet too, the children in many cases coming from long distances. Addresses by the above gentlemen were made to the Sunday-schools at several places on the route. Before reaching the fishing grounds a Sabbath was spent at a very pleasant village by the way, and the whole party will ever remember with unalloyed pleasure the way in which that day was spent. Some of the party attended church three times, assisting in the singing of the different churches. Addresses were made as before mentioned by Mr. Cooke and Mr. Page, and also by Mr. Reed, who is quite happy when he can talk to the little folks, and who does it well too, at the same time telling them what a large Sunday-school he has in Brooklyn, N. Y., in which he is deeply interested. Mr. Reed remarked that to his way of thinking, it was, as far as he was concerned, often a *means of grace*, to go on a fishing excursion; many seemed to agree with, while none ventured to differ from him in this view of the matter.

The last named gentlemen carried off all the honors for public speaking, none of the others of the party venturing to step forth, although urged to do so. They however contributed in various other ways, during the trip, to the general enjoyment, and the entire party without an exception, proved to the satisfaction of the people they came in contact with, that a fishing party *may* be made up of gentlemen, who will at all times remember to act as such, and still have a "jolly good time," thus setting an example that some fishing parties, notorious for license, rather than decorous frolic, may well follow with decided advantage to their reputations when abroad.

One more incident to Mr. Cooke's credit will bear relating before closing. How he did the thing it is difficult to surmise, but for thirty miles, Mr. C., traveling by the *Buggy*, in preference to the *White Eye* Line, pulled up at almost every house during the entire distance, for the purpose of distributing good little books in great variety, with colored covers, giving to each child (sometimes as many as 6 to a house,) three or four of the little volumes which children love to get, and become better for the reading thereof.

They will doubtless read these many times, as it will probably be a whole year before another generous missionary passes that way. The mystery of the thing is, how he could keep up the distribution, as he stopped at house after house and there were many on the way, and many, many children in the grand total, yet he had a full assortment for all the boys and girls and even for the babies, for the supply was inexhaustible. No one could see where he kept the large stock necessary for so extensive a journey; the only way to be imagined is, that before leaving home he must have tested to the utmost the capacity of every pocket in his coat, vest and pants, as well as those of his huge overcoat, for he seemed to deal out the books by the thousand, and yet,—the familiar and fatherly call would be, "*Come here my little darlings and get your books.*"

POLING UP OQUOSSOC RAPIDS.

## ADIEU.

Having now recorded the principal points of interest of this happy trip of the "Oquossoc Angling Association," the writer bids adieu to the scenes so much enjoyed, to the beautiful trout not the less admired that they escaped the barbéd hook, to all the kind friends with whom the glorious sport was shared, hoping next season to renew the manifold delights of the past one, and lastly to the courteous reader who has journeyed with us, in imagination, to the haunts of these giant trout of the Wilderness of Maine.

Sportively Yours,

(Original Designs by the Author.)

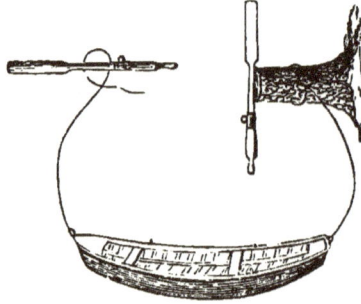

An ardent disciple of the good old Izaak.

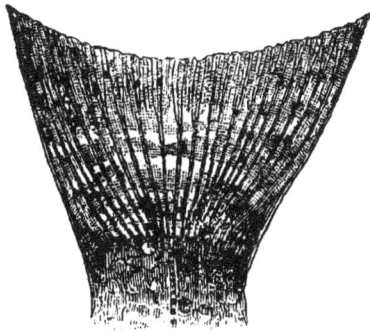

CAUDAL FINIS.

# ANDREW CLERK & CO.,

## 48 Maiden Lane & 35 Liberty Street,

## NEW YORK.

*Importers, Manufacturers and Dealers in all kinds of*

# Fishing Tackle, Fish Hooks, &c.,

### AND SOLE AGENTS OF

### WARRIN'S CELEBRATED

## Drilled Eyed & Telegraph Needles.

*We would call the attention of Anglers and Sportsmen in general, to our*

## Excelsior Split Bamboo Fly Rod,

*which is unequaled as to lightness, flexibility and strength. The most expert Anglers of the Adirondacks and Maine have bestowed upon us the highest encomiums, and not only upon* our *Excelsior Split Bamboo Rod,* but also upon our

## Cedar and Lancewood Rods,

*of which we have the largest and most complete variety in the world. In* **FLIES** *we have infinite varieties for which we are so justly celebrated and all of our own make. Also particular Flies for favorite localities, such as the Adirondacks, Maine, &c. All these are tied securely on the best silkworm gut, either tinted or plain, and have given the utmost satisfaction to Scientific Anglers. Our assortment of*

## Reels, Lines, Rods, Floats, Sinkers, &c., &c.,

*is unequaled, and too numerous to mention. To all lovers of the gentle art, we invite them to a close and careful inspection of our large and varied stock.*

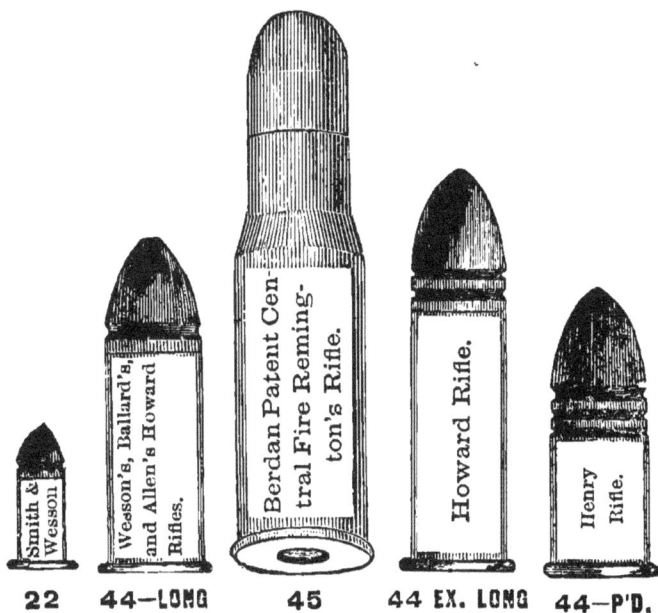

www.ingramcontent.com/pod-product-compliance
Lightning Source LLC
Chambersburg PA
CBHW021527270326
41930CB00008B/1126